The Journey Continues . . .

Healing for the Heart –
A Guide for Survival
In the
World of the Widow

Revised Edition

By Nancy E. Hughes

M.E.N.D. LLC PUBLISHING

M.E.N.D. LLC PUBLISHING

Copyright © 2017 by Nancy E. Hughes
All rights reserved. The author guarantees all contents are original and do not infringe upon the legal rights of any other person or work. No part of this book may be reproduced in any form without the permission of the author. The views expressed in this book are not necessarily those of the publisher.

Unless otherwise indicated, Bible quotations are taken from Ryrie Study Bible Expanded Edition. Copyright © 1984 by International Bible Society.

Cover Illustration by Andrea Fast

Dedicated . . .

To the beautiful women who graciously agreed to
share their journeys in the Widowhood Club.
I thank you.

To the millions of members in
this club who are
warriors every day.
I pray for you.

To my forever
best friend LeRoy.
I love you.

CONTENTS

INTRODUCTION 6

CHAPTER ONE 8
Nancy describes the decisions that need to be made in the world known as "widowhood" after becoming an instant member of this exclusive club without her permission.

CHAPTER TWO 22
Jacque was thrown violently into the widowhood club. She shares how to help children with the death of a parent and offers encouragement to those struggling on their journey.

CHAPTER THREE 34
Jeanette experienced shock and disbelief when she lost her husband to suicide. She describes the huge range of emotions and reactions that followed her sudden loss.

CHAPTER FOUR 48
Betty shares how to cope with the loss of a husband after 63 years of marriage to her best friend. She describes ways of getting through weeks and months after joining the club.

CHAPTER FIVE 62
Kay only had eight weeks to deal with the reality of losing her husband. She discusses being single in a "couples" world and finding love again.

CHAPTER SIX 78
Linda describes the struggle a widow can face as she tries to find hope and peace and healing when losing one's husband.

CHAPTER SEVEN 90
Jo was the mother of two small girls when she took her first breath as a widow. She shares lessons on dealing with grief as others depend on you for everything they need.

CHAPTER EIGHT 102
Debbie lost her husband while he was in the service in a foreign country. She shares the experience of her violent loss and her journey when she returned home to the U.S.

CHAPTER NINE 118
Saundra was suddenly dumped into the world of the widow. She addresses the loneliness that follows a widow and the comments from people who are not members of the club.

CHAPTER TEN 132
Jan and her husband had three children when he became ill and passed away just a few months later. She discusses the loss of her "rock" and how it affected all their lives.

CONCLUSION 148

SCRIPTURE REFERENCES 152

The Journey Continues . . .
Healing for the Heart –
A Guide for Survival
In the
World of the Widow

Introduction

This book is written for widows and for those wanting to offer encouragement to widows but unsure what to say or do – or not say or do. I began writing the first "Healing for the Heart" about four months after my husband LeRoy passed away in 2005. At first I simply wrote random thoughts concerning what I called "The Widowhood Club" and my being unceremoniously thrown into it without my permission and without instructions or explanations.

But I quickly learned that along with my unwanted membership I would repeatedly experience a wide range of emotions and situations that, without warning, could pull my heart high into the air as if I was riding on a Ferris wheel but drop it just as suddenly as the ride completed its circular motion near the ground. And if that was not enough, I also found after "they" became "she," my personal life changed completely. All because of a club. That I did not want to join.

It occurred to me that perhaps everything I was experiencing might also be very similar to what other widows faced as they too were initiated into widowhood. Perhaps not. So I contacted six women who were also widows like myself and asked them to share their experiences, which they all graciously agreed to do.

In this new revised edition of "Healing for the Heart," I have included three additional widows. Each one has a unique experience to share. The ladies you are going to read about have been members in the club from almost four years to over fifty years. They met the initiation requirements because of the loss of a spouse through sudden death, lingering health issues, accidents, military service or suicide. Left behind were wives, children, brothers and sisters, parents and friends whose lives were suddenly riddled with heartache, shattered dreams, confusion and a loss of security. "What do I do now?" the widow asks herself. "What can I do to help?" her friends ask each other.

It is my prayer that whether you are a widow or a friend wanting to support her, that you will find hope, encouragement and – yes – healing as these ten members of the widowhood club share their hearts and their journeys with you.

Chapter One

Nancy's journey begins...

Jeremiah 29:11 "For I know the plans I have for you," declares the Lord, "plans to prosper you and not to harm you, plans to give you hope and a future." (NIV)

Thrown into the club – but I don't want to join!

"He's gone, Nance…He's gone." My brother spoke those words with such precision and…something else…with a moan of hopelessness and helplessness melting into each other. My mind responds "Yes, I see, but please don't stop!" but the words won't come out. I try to say them, but my lips tremble and I feel my chin shaking silently. I can't take my eyes off the still form on our living room floor. He looks like he's taking a nap! How can that be?! My mind is racing while my thoughts scream to be heard! He can't be dead! But there he is. My brother is a doctor. I am a nurse. We've seen death before. And we both know that we are seeing it now. No more CPR. No more shocking. Stop the IV. Nothing is going to change what we see. My husband and best friend of 35 years, the one who made me laugh more than anyone else, the huge hands that reached to hold my slender ones, the smile, the deep voice that I could recognize in a room of a thousand . . . the love of my life had stepped before our Father with the snap of His fingers.

> "Listen, I tell you a mystery: We will not
> all sleep, but we will all be changed – in a flash,
> in the twinkling of an eye, at the last sound, the dead
> will be raised imperishable, and we will be changed."
> I Corinthians 15:51-52 (NIV)

++++++++++++++++++++++

What are the rules?

The day my husband LeRoy died, people were all over my house . . . hundreds, I am told. A room full of people no matter where I turned: the living room, kitchen, bedroom. Kind people, loving people, people who were in shock just as I was over my loss. Some were crying. Some were just shaking their heads as if to say "How can this be?" while others thoughtfully carried in armfuls of paper products and food.

We as a nation are programmed to celebrate every bit of news that comes our way – good OR bad – with food. Eat because of a birthday, or because of a new job or because of stress or because of NO stress…but eat! I did not want to eat. I only wanted one thing – that my husband could be with me – but that was not going to happen anymore. Ever. End of discussion.

However, people kept putting food before me. "Eat, Nancy, you need to eat." (No, I don't. I need to throw up. I need to scream. I need my husband. But I do NOT need to eat.) "Here, just a sandwich. I will NOT leave until you eat."

Quietly but firmly the minister who was going to do the service said to no one in particular and yet to everyone: "Nancy doesn't need to eat. She's not going to faint from not having a meal or two. Just make sure she drinks water. Nothing more."

His glance at me spoke volumes. His experience as a minister had taught him that not everybody reacts to stress by eating.

Some people react exactly opposite. And it's okay. But we lose a tremendous amount of water when we cry and we all must have water to survive.

> "Jesus answered, "Everyone who drinks this water will be thirsty again, but whoever drinks the water I give him will never thirst."
> John 4:13, 14a (NIV)

+++++++++++++++++++++

Am I "over it" yet?

Several months after my club membership began, I received a call from a caring person concerning a mutual friend who had also lost her husband. "She comes to work crying, she cries off and on during the day, she leaves crying." was the comment. "Can you talk to her? It needs to get better."

It struck me as rather odd that I, a recent widow, would be contacted to talk to another recent widow, about getting it all together and moving on with life. I wondered why? Could it be that, because I do not happen to cry in public over my loss, it is assumed that I am now healed of my grief?

There is a perception that grief is like a bad cold: 10 days and some TLC and it is over. Not so. Not so. I may grieve the rest of my life over the loss of my husband. Oh, life will go on. And I will go on. That's my choice. And that's God's plan.

But allow me to show you my hurt and my tears once in a while. And some day, I will allow you to show me yours.

"He will wipe every tear from their eyes. There will be no more
death Or mourning or crying or pain, for the old
order of things has passed away."
Revelation 21:4 (NIV)
++++++++++++++++++++++

My strength is gone.

The evening my husband passed away, everyone finally left our home about midnight and I fell into bed. I had felt compelled to stay up until the last person left in order to show everyone that I was strong and I would be okay. To say that I was exhausted does not begin to cover how I felt, but the shock of the last several hours glossed over that exhaustion and smothered it in numbness.

I laid on my right side, looking over at my husband's pillow, but unable to focus because of the tears. Sleep did not find me during those hours but it was replaced by something else: along with the incredible sadness that I felt was an even more incredible peace that I simply cannot describe.

My eyes did not close that night but neither did my Father's. I stayed on His lap all night as He held me in His arms. I could hear His voice over and over: "I am still in control. I have a plan. Trust me, Nancy, trust me."

When my sadness gave way to extreme exhaustion and I could hold on no longer, my Father held on to me. And He did not let go.

"He will cover you with his feathers, and under his wings you will find refuge. . ."
Psalm 91:4 (NIV)

++++++++++++++++++++++

Advice can be adverse.

The advice that one receives in "the club" of widowhood can be of extreme value or it can just be extreme. Well-meaning people want, more than anything, to help.

One particular lady approached me about a month after my husband passed away. She leaned over to me, as if sharing wisdom meant only for my ears, and with a pat on my hand, she said "You lost your husband? Get a dog."

Now, I am quite certain that my face had a look closely akin to "Are you nuts?" on it, but I simply said "Thank you so much for your advice." She nodded, smiled and walked away, knowing in her heart that she had made my life perfect again.

I stared at her back thinking, "Husband and a dog, husband and a dog. How in the world are they similar?" It occurred to me that they both eat on demand and you have to clean up after them on a daily basis.

Could that have been what she meant? I haven't asked. And I doubt that I will. Some questions are better left unanswered.

" . . . Has God not made foolish the wisdom of the world?"
I Corinthians 1:20 (NIV)

++++++++++++++++++++

What's in a name?

When you become a member of "the club," you automatically become a name dropper. I'm not talking about someone who is quick to mention the name of a famous person as if they are best friends: "Well, I had lunch at Nick's Place and I sat at a table
next to the president of the bank…well, I THINK he was…or at least he had the same hair."

Name dropping, to a widow, means that she is immediately encouraged to take her husband's name off any and all documents and papers they possessed together. I went to an appointment with my insurance agent. I had sold a seldom used car and needed to let them know. The agent said "While you are here, do you want to take your husband's name off the insurance?" A very innocent question. A question asked in kindness.

I must be ambidextrous because my mind said "NO! I do NOT want his name off the policy. One more way to erase him from my life!" while simultaneously my mouth was saying "Yes, that's a good idea. Thank you." The look of pain on my face caused the agent to quickly add "It doesn't have to be done right now. It can wait a while if you wish." I'm sure it was a good idea. Just not to me.

Yet another name dropping incident occurred: my husband had been gone 32 weeks and I was on my last pad of checks. As I looked at them…"LeRoy OR Nancy Hughes"…I could not bring myself to order checks without his name. Maybe next time. But not this time.

It is okay to leave your husband's name in the phone book or on checks or even on return address stickers. It is also okay to change them if you wish. There is an issue of safety and protection if the name remains. But it is not an issue of the law. Do as you so desire.

"The name of the Lord is a strong tower;
the righteous run to it and are safe."
Proverbs 18:10 (NIV)

++++++++++++++++++++++

I don't need boxes – yet.

A friend who meant well called me a few days after my husband's funeral. "I'll be over tomorrow and we'll get rid of LeRoy's clothes," she said. I couldn't help my immediate response: "Why? Why would I do that?" She continued "They will be a constant reminder that he is gone. Every time you look at them you will be reminded of his death. It's much better to get rid of them."

My friend has not lost her husband. I tell her as kindly as I can that I have no immediate plans to get rid of his clothes. Maybe later I will do that. Goodwill always needs things. But not right now. She seems to be satisfied with that answer and we hang up.

What I don't tell her is that I go into my closet, sit on the floor, and bury my face in his shirts. And cry? Yes, I cry. I grieve. I'm not a masochist, inflicting pain intentionally on myself. I'm pulling his shirts to my face because they smell like him…and I will keep all his clothes until they no longer carry his scent. Then…maybe then…I will give them away.

> "Blessed are those who mourn,
> for they shall be comforted."
> Matthew 5:4 (NIV)

++++++++++++++++++++

Nancy's journey continues . . .

It has been twelve years since Nancy was thrown into the Widowhood Club. She shares her experiences with other women who are widows through speaking at women's groups and by writing in the hope that they might receive encouragement from her about the widowhood journey.

As she looks back, Nancy is able to see the progress she has made in her journey of grieving. Perhaps two steps back but three forward – such a change from the weeks and months after her loss. And yet, there are days when the backward steps far outnumber the forward ones. And it is okay.

She still receives occasional advice from non-members of the club and is able to thank each person and go on. She determines her personal decisions; for example, Nancy waited about three years after he passed away to remove her husband's name from her checks and the phone book.

Two years ago she had her husband's shirts made into blankets for her children and grandchildren and gave the other clothes to family members and to Good Will. She still has days when tears quietly slip down her cheeks but she shares "I am confident that the Lord will continue to be faithful in all things. He has never left my side and He never will."

"Have I not commanded you? Be strong and courageous.

Do not be terrified, do not be discouraged,

for the Lord your God will be

with you wherever you go."

Joshua 1:9 (NIV)

++++++++++++++++++++++

Holding on...

If you are a widow, can you identify with Nancy and the thoughts she has shared? Journal your feelings, thoughts and encouraging Scriptures here.

_____
_____
_____
_____
_____
_____
_____
_____
_____
_____
_____

By her side...

If you are a friend to a widow, can you identify with the help that Nancy has shared? Journal your feelings, thoughts and encouraging Scriptures here.

_____
_____
_____
_____
_____
_____
_____
_____
_____
_____
_____
_____
_____

Chapter Two

Jacque's journey begins...

Song of Solomon 2:8-17: "Listen! My lover! Look! Here he comes, leaping across the mountains, bounding over the hills.
My lover is like a gazelle or a young stag. Look!...See!
The winter is past; the rains are over and gone. Flowers appear on the earth;
the season of singing has come, the cooing of doves is heard in our land...
My lover is mine and I am his; he browses among the lilies.
Until the day breaks and the shadows flee, turn, my lover, and be like a gazelle or
like a young stag on the rugged hills." (NIV)

This can't be happening!

It was one of those marriages that many dream about but few ever actually find. Jacque is petite with dark hair and a ready smile - a pretty young woman who can't help but laugh at her husband as he plans joke after joke just to see that smile. He is a devoted husband and father and his family comes before his job or his hobbies of hunting and fishing. Their son is 2 ½ years old and they just found out the previous week that this tiny life Jacque has been carrying for 4 ½ months is a girl – exactly what her husband had prayed for! Life could not be better or more blessed. Then on a fall afternoon as her husband was hunting, Jacque's cell phone rang: "Honey, I've been shot." Her first reaction was the same as almost every other time he has played a joke on her: "Yeah, right." But instantly the line went dead, so she called him back. In a split second, with the force of a searing hot knife being thrust into her heart, Jacque realized that this was no joke but the beginning moments of a horrible nightmare come true. A few hours later she found herself sitting next to her husband's bed in the intensive care unit at the hospital, holding his hand as she whispered her love. From somewhere near her shoulder a doctor quietly told her that there was nothing further they can do to stop her husband's bleeding. A day that began like so many others ended at 9:04 p.m. for Jacque's husband and for her as well. The bleeding in his body could not be stopped. The bleeding in her heart had only begun.

> "My flesh and my heart may fail, but God is the strength of my heart and my portion forever."
> Psalm 73:26 (NIV)

++++++++++++++++++++

Asking hurts and helps.

"People stop asking how you are doing," Jacque says. "It's not that they don't want to know. They care very much. They just believe that by asking, they are opening up a painful injury again and again."

Friends, acquaintances, family – you remember my husband. You picture the laughing, teasing, always-helping-others, bigger-than-life man. And you saw him with me and our son. You saw the love in his eyes and in his actions and the identical response in mine. So you know I am hurting.

But please ask me how I am! Yes, it hurts. Yes, it is unbelievably hard. Yes, I am always looking up, expecting him to walk through the door. Yes, I pray for strength to get though every minute of every day.

But something else occurs when you inquire: your kindness helps my heart, ever so slightly, to begin to mend. And to heal.

"Therefore, as God's chosen people, holy and dearly loved,
clothe yourselves with compassion, kindness,
humility, gentleness and patience."
Colossians 3:12 (NIV)

++++++++++++++++++++++

Telling my children

Jacque's son was only 2 ½ years old when his father died. He had no concept of death but simply knew that Daddy was not at their home any more. Jacque told him that his daddy was now living with the angels and, if you ask her son that is exactly what he says.

When they go to the cemetery he always yells "Hi Daddy!" as he brings gifts of flowers and a pinwheel to the gravesite. "That way," Jacque says, "he sees the wind blowing the pinwheel and knows that his daddy hears him."

You may have ideas concerning how to explain to my children what has happened to their father. They do not need philosophy and long explanations. They simply need to know about God's love and that He watches over them.

Please let me be the one to answer their questions. If I cannot find an answer, I will look to you for advice.

> "(God is)…A father to the fatherless,
> a defender of widows."
> Psalm 68:5 (NIV)

++++++++++++++++++++

Laughter does not mean healing.

Jacque states that one of her husband's best friends said the only way he has made it through this loss was to see her smile once in a while – even though it might be a "fake" smile.

It is not required that you laugh or smile in the "Widowhood Club." Indeed, it is an almost impossible feat. Just know that my laughter, if you hear it, is harder on me than on you. I feel guilty.

I am in a state of duel membership: One part of me wants to return to a more normal life and yes, to smile. Yet the other part is crying day and night over my loss.

As time moves on, other decisions become harder and harder. "Do I go out to eat?" Will someone see me and think that I am "over" my loss? "Didn't she just lose her husband?" they will say. Should I take off my wedding rings? My hand is naked without them. My heart is broken without him. I buy a new dress. But why? My husband will not be there to tell me how great I look…even if I don't.

Bear with me as I travel this new path the Lord is designing for me. He knows my name…and my heart.

> "Even in laughter the heart may ache,
> and joy may end in grief."
> Proverbs 14:13 (NIV)

++++++++++++++++++++++

May I ask you something?

"I reached a point when I realized that I could not do everything by myself," Jacque said. "I knew I needed help."

There are people everywhere, including friends, family, church family and simple acquaintances who are waiting in the wings to help you.

Eaves need to be cleaned out, lawns mowed, oil changed, furniture moved, trees cut down, meetings kept, babysitters called, bills paid, plants watered, boards replaced, rooms painted, food cooked, Christmas lights strung, laundry folded, gardens tilled, prayers lifted.

Wonderful people are waiting…thinking… "If only she will ask." So ask.

> "Ask and it will be given to you; seek and you will find; knock and the door will be opened to you."
> Matthew 7:7 (NIV)

++++++++++++++++++++

I can't repay but I will try.

Jacque was overwhelmed by the outpouring of love and support when her husband died. She received hundreds of cards and letters.

At the funeral, 16 fellow hunters and good friends stood as the eulogy was being read – united in their grief and love for this man. A special auction was held to raise money for the family and a memorial was set up in his name. Meals, baby gifts, cases of diapers, and donations from companies around town as well as from total strangers poured in.

As widows, we cannot begin to express our gratitude for what you have done and continue to do for us. We may miss writing a "thank you" card for the food you brought or the lovely flowers at the funeral or the books of stamps you sent with an encouraging letter. We may forget to tell you how thoughtful your note was to us on a day we really needed it or how much we appreciate the lawn being mowed.

But please understand that our children will know about you because we will tell them how you shared your lives with ours. And your love.

> "I have not stopped giving thanks for you,
> remembering you in my prayers."
> Ephesians 1:16 (NIV)

++++++++++++++++++++++

The new normal isn't - yet . . .

There are days when Jacque is able to find the "normal" in her routine and other days when it simply doesn't exist. Life seems to mimic an acrobat in a circus ring as he struggles to keep plates spinning on top of poles – all in unison. If a plate crashes to the floor, he simply grabs another one and continues. She does not have that luxury.

Today a co-worker remarks that Jacque has been gone a lot. She does not realize that Jacque's plates – the loss of her husband, problems with her pregnancy, spending extra time with her small son – are all demanding to be spun at the same time. The spinning plate of work is not a priority compared to her small son's anxiety and, for now, it must crash to the ground.

If that happens, please come alongside us and pick up the broken pieces. Better yet, offer to take care of our spinning plates of less importance during this transition to new normal.

> "Two are better than one, because they have a
> good return for their work; If one falls down,
> his friend can help him up. But pity the man who
> falls and has no one to help him up!"
> Ecclesiastes 4:9-10 (NIV)

++++++++++++++++++++

Jacque's journey continues . . .

"I have survived," Jacque shares, "but I believe life without Mike is harder than ever now." When her husband passed away, her son was 2 ½ and her daughter not yet born. They are now ages 12 and 15 and Jacque is the only parent to help them with everything in their lives, from homework to band concerts to gymnastics to driving lessons to solving girl drama. And with goodnight kisses.

She sees her husband in both her children: her son has his handsome features and her daughter inherited his teasing personality. She prays daily for guidance in helping them make choices in their lives and often thinks of how proud their dad would be of them.

"People often ask me how I do it," she says. "And I tell them that I have to! I wasn't given a choice in this so I now choose to make the most of my situation." Jacque will tell you that it is hard and there are still nights when she cries herself to sleep but her love for the Lord and her children keep her going every day.

"The Lord himself goes before you and will be
with you; he will never leave you nor forsake you.
Do not be afraid; do not be discouraged."
Deuteronomy 31:8 (NIV)
+++++++++++++++++++++++

Holding on . . .

If you are a widow, can you identify with Jacque and the thoughts she has shared? Journal your feelings, thoughts and encouraging Scriptures here.

By her side . . .

If you are a friend to a widow, can you identify with the help that Jacque has shared? Journal your feelings, thoughts and encouraging Scriptures here.

_____
_____
_____
_____
_____
_____
_____
_____
_____
_____

Chapter Three

Jeanette's journey begins . . .

Psalm 91:1 "He who dwells in the shelter of the Most High will rest in the shadow
of the Almighty. I will say of the Lord, "He is my refuge" and my fortress, my God,
in whom I trust." (NIV)

Shock in the loss.

The heartbreak of losing a husband suddenly to disease or an accident shatters the stability and security for any woman. But when that loss is due to suicide, the blackness that covers the life of his wife and family left behind cannot be intelligently described. The question of "why" jumps out of the shadows again and again, ambushing and piercing the fragile hearts of those attacked. This is the world that Jeanette was forced into as she came home from church one Sunday morning to find that her husband had made the decision to take his life. She was not prepared for what lay ahead; but then, who could be?

"I have great sorrow and unceasing

anguish in my heart."

Romans 9:2 (NIV)

++++++++++++++++++++

How am I supposed to look?

It must be the consensus of friends and family that something needs to be said concerning a widow's appearance in the days following her loss.

"Several people came up to me after my husband died and said 'You look so good!'" Jeanette recalls. "I kept wondering how I was supposed to look. Disheveled? No makeup? Totally blank look on my face? What?"

Still others commented that they could tell by looking at her that she was "such a strong woman!"

I have no idea how I looked after my husband's death because my one priority was to keep breathing. I'm not sure I can even tell you what I wore to the funeral. Honestly, none of that matters. The one thing I do know, however, is that my heart was being held by the God who knows me better than anyone, from the inside out.

"Search me, O God, and know my heart; test me and
Know my anxious thoughts."
Psalm 139:23 (NIV)
+++++++++++++++++++++

That doesn't make me feel better.

When someone passes away, it can be very difficult to know what to say to comfort those left behind. We are so sad for the loss and truly want to say something – anything – to ease their heartache.

However, in our haste to find the "right words" when a spouse has committed suicide, we struggle, and rightly so. There is no cancer, no car accident, no specific event that one can point to and say "There. That's why he died" because often the reason behind the suicide is never known.

So we say what we think are words of comfort, not realizing that those words are doing more to damage than benefit a fragile wife.

Jeanette had not one, but two people who made the same comment to her after she lost her husband: "I am glad it wasn't murder/suicide." That was a situation she had never contemplated – until she heard their words.

Please resist the urge to share your opinions about what could have been concerning the circumstances surrounding my husband's death. Rather, simply tell me that you are sorry or that you are praying for me.

Before you speak one word, put yourself in my place and decide how you would feel if the very words you are getting ready to speak to me were spoken to you.

"Do not be quick with your mouth, do not be hasty
in your heart to utter anything before God.
God is in heaven and you are on earth,
so let your words be few."
Ecclesiastes 5:2 (NIV)
++++++++++++++++++++++

Enough anger for a lifetime.

The day Jeanette's husband committed suicide she was in shock and total disbelief. And then the anger came at what he had done, not just to himself but to her and other family and friends. She said "I loved him so much and felt so betrayed by what he had done that I took my wedding rings off and never put them back on – even for the visitation and funeral."

One week after the funeral the shock and anger intensified. That week became two and continued through one, two and three months. The anger would often build and be smothered with disbelief and heartache. And something else began to creep in: feelings of guilt at not somehow seeing that something was wrong in her husband's life. He hadn't felt well. Was there something more that she should have picked up on? Then the anger would roll over her again and the cycle would repeat itself.

The anger and disbelief that I feel over my husband's death may honestly last a lifetime. When a marriage of 34 years ends suddenly and permanently without explanation, emotions are tossed about like a small boat in a massive storm.

When those emotions threaten to take over my every moment, I will lay them down at the foot of the cross and call to my Father. And He will answer.

"Hear my prayer, O Lord; listen to my cry for mercy.

In the day of my trouble I will call to you.

For you will answer me."

Psalm 86.6 (NIV)

++++++++++++++++++++

No longer my home.

Jeanette felt almost immediately that she needed to move from her home after her husband committed suicide there. "Every day as I walked through the house I would relive in my mind the scene I found when I came home that morning," she said.

Where once there was laughter and conversation, the home instead became lonely and depressing. When her mind wandered back to that day, Jeanette would immediately make herself think of something else or she would take on a task – any task – to try to replace the ache in her heart and mind.

But it still became unbearable to stay there so she put her house on the market. "The selling of 'our house' could help me begin to heal from an incredibly sad chapter in my life," she said "and help me to be able to open a new chapter at a different location."

My decision to move from my home because of my husband's death does not mean I am running away from my past. It simply means I am choosing to go in a different direction.

"Simon Peter answered him, 'Lord, to whom shall we go?
You have the words of eternal life."
John 6:68 (NIV)

++++++++++++++++++++++

Why's and if only's.

After her husband's death, Jeanette visited the cemetery at least one or two times a week. "I sat there, crying my eyes out and asking him 'Why did you do this to me?' and 'How could you do this to yourself?' and asking God "Why? Why?" over and over.

Anger, guilt, shock and an extreme sadness came in waves, relentlessly and viciously. And each wave carried an undercurrent swirling with "if only's."

If only he had explained to me what was going on. If only I had known what he was about to do. If only I had stayed home that day. If only. If only.

I realize that many of my questions over my husband's death cannot be answered. But I also know that our God is a big enough Father to handle any questions that I have as I grieve and mourn this loss. He hears every question, every cry, every moan. And He understands every tear I shed, every question I ask and every regret in my heart.

Nowhere in Scripture does God promise us that we will receive all the answers to our "why" questions here on earth. But He does promise that, no matter what journey we are on, He will never leave us.

Not long ago I watched dozens of balloons being released, one at a time, to honor a special event. Please know that in the same way I will release my "why's" and "if only's" to the Lord and allow

Him to cover me in His mercy and love. He knows the answers to my questions . . . and some day I will, too.

> "Let us then approach the throne of grace with
> confidence, so that we may receive mercy
> and find grace to help us in our
> time of need."
> Hebrews 4:16 (NIV)

++++++++++++++++++++++

Starting over.

"Starting over has its personal challenges," Jeanette shares. "It feels so strange to date again and to have another person in your life after being married for 34 years." And how much do you share as you get to know him?

"If I'm having a particularly down day, I don't feel it is fair to burden him by sharing the reasons for those feelings." Simply dating again after being married doesn't seem quite right.

And there is a concern about what people will think. "I often feel that when people see me dating, the first thing they think about is that I am the woman whose husband killed himself."

This starting over period is so hard, to say the least. If you see me on a date, please know that I am simply trying to bring some normalcy again to my life.

I cannot change what has happened in the past. But with guidance from the Lord, I can trust Him with the direction of my future.

> "Trust in the Lord with all your heart and lean not
> on your own understanding. In all your ways
> acknowledge him and he will make
> your paths straight."
> Proverbs 3:5-6 (NIV)

++++++++++++++++++++

Jeanette's journey continues . . .

"Since the passing of my husband, I have come to the conclusion that there is no "closure" as many people talk about," Jeanette shares. But even though it seems as though this wound of suicide may never heal, she has learned how to go on with her life.

That does not mean that she has forgotten her late husband or the circumstances surrounding his death. What it does mean is that she has chosen to hold on to the Lord through every moment of the storm roaring around her and when her strength is gone, to allow Him to hold on to her and never let go.

Jeanette says that she has learned that, when someone dies, one should never ask the surviving spouse or family member how they passed away. "Just say you are sorry for the loss and leave it at that. If the surviving spouse wants you to know, she will tell you."

She reconnected with her college sweetheart and they began dating and became engaged. Jeanette was resistant to marriage again but, after becoming deathly ill, she decided as she began to recuperate that God had truly saved her for a reason and that her fiancé was part of His plan. They were married soon after.

"There is a silver lining in every dark cloud," she says. "I have a beautiful marriage to a wonderful man, my health is good, and I praise the Lord every day for answering my prayers and for never leaving my side."

"The Lord is my rock, my fortress and my deliverer;
my God is my rock, in whom I take refuge.
He is my shield and the horn of my
salvation, my stronghold."

Psalm 18:2 (NIV)

++++++++++++++++++++++

Holding on . . .

If you are a widow, can you identify with Jeanette and the thoughts she has shared? Journal your feelings, thoughts and encouraging Scriptures here.

_____

_____

_____

_____

_____

_____

_____

_____

_____

_____

_____

_____

By her side...

If you are a friend to a widow, can you identify with the help that Jeanette has shared? Journal your feelings, thoughts and encouraging Scriptures here.

_____
_____
_____
_____
_____
_____
_____
_____
_____
_____
_____
_____
_____

Chapter Four

Betty's journey begins...

Isaiah 41:13: "For I am the Lord, your God, who takes hold of your right hand and says to you, Do not fear; I will help you." (NIV)

Gently losing a lifetime.

Standing in the hospital room, looking at her husband of 63 years as he slept in his clean, antiseptic bed, Betty knew that their marriage here on earth was soon coming to an end. His health had not been as good as they had hoped after his open heart surgery. Now, after 2 ½ months in hospitals, there was no surprise or shock as the end came quietly – only an immense sadness that this man who was bigger than life to so many and loved by even more would no longer be a part of their lives here on earth. It could be argued that there should not be as much grief at this loss as, perhaps, a couple who had only been married a few months or years. However, there is an indescribable loneliness that descends quickly when the person you ate your meals with at 6:00 a.m., noon and 6:00 p.m. every day, the one who shared the same home with you for over 60 years, the one who knew what you were going to say before you said it, the one to whom you could tell absolutely anything and know that he would never repeat it to another . . . that person is no longer at your side or a part of your life. Betty's membership into the club began in such a fashion.

"He heals the brokenhearted and
binds up their wounds."
Psalm 147:3 (NIV)
++++++++++++++++++++

The best of friends.

Betty says that one friend in particular, a close friend, has gotten her through the very rough days and months after her husband's death.

"I was invited out with a group of friends that my husband and I always went with and I found myself as a single in a room of couples. It was very hard." But, Betty continues, her friend, who knew she was going with the group of couples, sensed her heavy heart and emotional sadness.

"I could not have been home more than 10 minutes," Betty said, "when the phone rang. It was Sue." "I just knew tonight had to be very hard for you and that you needed to talk," the voice on the phone said. She understood that her best friend had a need and wanted to be there for her.

If you are my best friend, then you know me better than anyone. Allow me some time and space but do not be afraid to call on me as often as you sense I need that call. Being willing to step into my sadness makes us even closer.

"... there is a friend who sticks closer than a brother."
Proverbs 18:24 (NIV)

++++++++++++++++++++

Who cares?

Activities that Betty says were such a part of her life for years became unimportant when her husband passed away. It was simply because the majority of them involved him.

"For a while, all I could think was 'Why entertain?' 'Who cares about the garden?' 'Golfing with friends…no, thank you.'" Betty stated.

When the person that we shared our day's activities with for years is no longer with us, we may think "Why bother?"

Please encourage me to participate in those things that I used to do…golfing, playing bridge, tennis. Just remember that, for me, the rules have changed. And I will have to adapt without my doubles partner. All the things I used to do may seem pointless to me. Not forever. But for now.

> ". . . weeping may remain for a night,
> but rejoicing comes in the morning."
> Psalm 30:5b (NIV)

++++++++++++++++++++

Just make the offer.

When the last friend has left, the last hug has been offered, the last tear has been shed and I am alone in my home, offer to stay with me. I may need you to stay…I may not. But please make the offer and allow me to make that decision.

Betty says that she was amazed at the outpouring of invitations from family and friends to stay with her after her husband's death. "My grandchildren, even my great grandchildren, wanted to stay with me. It gave me such comfort in having them there."

Some members of the club feel they can make the move forward to stay by themselves from the beginning. Others want someone there to buffer the silence and loss for a while. I may tell you I am okay by myself and that could very well be true, but just in case I call in the middle of the night, please have your suitcase ready.

I am not asking you to take up permanent residence with me but I AM asking you to step into my world – just for a while – as I learn to adjust to a new life and lifestyle without my husband.

"But if a widow has children or grandchildren,
these should learn first of all to put their religion
into practice by caring for their own family
and so repaying their parents and grandparents,
for this is pleasing to God."
I Timothy 5:4 (NIV)

++++++++++++++++++++++

Eventually, yes I can.

The time will come when I am able to focus less on my needs and more on the needs of others. But please understand that right now I need this time of healing to gain strength. Strength from the Lord that I must have in order to someday reach out to the growing number of club members around me.

There will come a point in my grief when I am able to look beyond myself and reach out to others who are hurting from the same emotional pain of loss that I have experienced. And I will begin to see that there are other people like me who are hurting and need understanding, compassion and hope.

There is healing in the realization that I can perhaps, in some small way, help to soothe a broken heart or encourage a lonely sister in the club…because I have been there. This process of gaining strength may take weeks or months or even years. But it will happen.

>"(God) who comforts us in all our troubles,
>so that we can comfort those in any trouble
>with the comfort we ourselves
>have received from God."
>II Corinthians 1:4 (NIV)

++++++++++++++++++++++

Are you a member, too?

If you have become a member of this club before me, then more than anyone, you truly know how I am feeling and what I am facing. Please call me. Just knowing that you have entered the pit previously and are slowly but surely climbing out will give me tremendous comfort and encouragement…and hope.

For Betty, having a friend who had "been there" and had already been inducted into the club was a great help to her. "She knew what I was feeling and, at times, exactly what I was thinking because she had taken the steps before me," Betty shares.

If you have lost your husband, please send a note or make a phone call to me. So many people say they know how I feel, but they are not members.

They do not understand why I cry when I see a certain food in the supermarket or hear a song on the radio or smell cologne in the men's section of the department store. They are unable to fathom that these simple things remind me of my husband and the life we shared together…and the loss that separates us now.

I need you to reassure me that, while you are also grieving, you have walked this path and you are surviving. And I need to know from you that I, too, will follow in your footsteps and survive.

"A cheerful look brings joy to the heart, and good news gives health to the bones."
Proverbs 15:30 (NIV)

++++++++++++++++++++

We all cope differently with loss.

Betty found it hard to do some of her everyday routines. She and her husband shared meals at the dining room table but, as Betty says, "I found myself standing and eating at the kitchen counter instead. I could not get used to sitting by myself each meal."

Another difference for Betty was her husband's recliner. "I used to sit across the room from him as we exchanged glances and smiles or conversations as we watched television together. But after he passed away, I sat in his chair so I didn't have to look at where he used to be."

Nighttime was also especially hard, Betty says. "So I slept on my husband's side of the bed. Instead of reaching for him, I was already in "his" spot."

Please know that these changes may not make sense to you if you are not in the "Widowhood Club." But to those of us who are members, each tiny difference helps us to manage the new event or routine that comes to us in the best way we know how at the moment.

> "You, O Lord, keep my lamp burning;
> my God turns my darkness into light."
> Psalm 18:28 (NIV)

++++++++++++++++++++

Betty's journey continues . . .

"After my husband passed away twelve years ago, I chose to continue living in the home we had built together," Betty shares.

She states that very day there is something that reminds her of their many years together. "I believe that although life is never the same after losing someone who was part of your life for so long, the world goes on and one does adjust to living alone."

Betty continues a close relationship with her family and they all still live in her home town. She also has a close relationship with old friends and has made many new friendships.

. "I am active in my church, visiting in the nursing home, PEO, bridge clubs and visiting on the telephone," she comments. "The secret of a happy and fulfilled life is keeping busy and thinking of others."

". . . being confident of this, that he who began
A good work in you will carry it on to completion
until the day of Christ Jesus."
Philippians 1:6 (NIV)

++++++++++++++++++++

Holding on . . .

If you are a widow, can you identify with Betty and the thoughts she has shared? Journal your feelings, thoughts and encouraging Scriptures here.

By her side . . .

If you are a friend to a widow, can you identify with the help that Betty has shared? Journal your feelings, thoughts and encouraging Scriptures here.

_____
_____
_____
_____
_____
_____
_____
_____
_____
_____
_____

Chapter Five

Kay's journey begins . . .

Proverbs 31:25 "She is clothed with strength and dignity; she can laugh at the days to come." (NIV)

In tune until the end.

Kay became a bride at 16 years of age. Her husband was big and strong and could move mountains in her eyes. She went from living at home with her parents to marriage to this man and then children four years later. Her husband owned several horses and was known and highly respected throughout the community and beyond. Side by side they worked raising horses and children, cultivating crops and love. After 31 years of marriage, Kay and her husband were very much in tune with each other's every thought and glance and smile. That is why Kay knew without her husband speaking a word that he was not feeling well and hadn't for some time. She finally convinced him to go to the hospital for a checkup. The news was sudden and suffocating: "You have cancer and you have about 8 weeks to live." But wait! That's not how it's supposed to be! Kay's mind began to spin as she looked at her children and her husband...her life! The doctors were not wrong. Within 8 weeks, Kay was thrown out of her couple's world. Everything comes in two's . . . but Kay would very quickly face the world – and join the widowhood club – as one.

> " . . . He has sent me to bind up
> the brokenhearted . . ."
> Isaiah 61:1 (NIV)

++++++++++++++++++++

Do not count my tears.

If you do not see tears from me at the funeral, please do not mistake that for an absence of caring. You have no idea what I have has been through before that event and how many tears I have already shed. Or how many more I will shed in private, alone.

Kay's husband spent the last 8 weeks of his life in a hospital and a wheelchair. She says "At the end, there was a relief in me at knowing that he was no longer suffering. I was unable to cry at the funeral because I knew that, for him, the pain and suffering were over."

Watching a loved one dying with an incurable disease is similar to watching the wind blowing the sparks of a fire out of control. You see it happening but you realize as you put out three small embers that three more have sprung up and no matter how hard you try, you are not going to be able to stop the inevitable destruction.

It was not until two weeks after the funeral that the reality of her husband's death hit her. "He's really not coming back!" her mind suddenly screamed. She stated that she began crying and those tears continued for days, weeks, months and years.

Although outwardly I may appear calm after my loss, do not assume that the inside follows suit.

"... The Lord does not look at the things man looks at. Man looks at the outward appearance, but the Lord looks at the heart."
I Samuel 16:7 (NIV)

++++++++++++++++++++++

Do you really hear me?

What I say might not be as important as what I don't say. Allow the ears of your heart to listen for the unspoken words of mine.

You ask me how I'm doing after the loss of my husband and I say "Fine." While that is what you hear with your physical ears, you know with your spiritual ears that my answer is not completely truthful.

Maybe for this moment in this hour of this day, "fine" might cover how I am feeling. But overall, it is merely a prepared answer to a question that is asked of me almost daily.

Rather than ask me how I'm doing, let me know that you are praying for me. That you think of me often. That you want to take me out for coffee next Tuesday. Allow me the opportunity to expand on "fine" and to tell you how I am truly feeling.

> "If a man shuts his ears to the
> cry of the poor, he too will cry
> out and not be answered."
> Proverbs 21:13 (NIV)

++++++++++++++++++++

Remind me to breathe.

I am a passenger on a boat with no oars. The water is either calm or it is crashing and threatening to submerge everything in its path – including me. I never know when the waves will hit so there is no way for me to prepare you for what you may see. Just be ready to throw me a rope…or at least a paddle.

One day I may seem perfectly "okay" to you. I may be at the supermarket shopping and you notice that I am humming quietly to myself. You think "She's just fine. She is moving on. Things are so much better." You may even mention that in conversation with your friends.

The very next day, you may see me in a store and you cannot deny the look of loneliness on my face and the tears threatening to break free. You are perplexed! Is this not the same woman who, only yesterday, was humming? Who seemed to be "getting over" her loss? What in the world is wrong? Nothing. Nothing is wrong at all.

On the first day that you saw me, I was in a pool of calm water. I was able to sit on the cushion in the middle of the boat and relax for a few minutes. But the second day? Oh, the second day was one in which the waves struck suddenly without warning and tossed me out of the boat and into the water with such force that I had to fight for air and hold on with the last ounce of strength that I had.

When you see me and know that I am struggling to breathe and keep my head above the waves, lift me up to the One who controls water with a word and my life with His love. He is the only life preserver that I need.

> "…Then he got up and rebuked the
> winds and the waves, and it
> was completely calm."
> Matthew 8:26 (NIV)

+++++++++++++++++++++

Do I try again?

Someday I may choose to date again. That does not mean that my grieving is over. That does not mean that I really didn't love my husband. It DOES mean that I am considering canceling my membership in the club and joining the world of couples once again. Nothing more.

After 12 years of being single, Kay says that she began to pray regularly that the Lord would send her someone that she could share her life with and who shared her beliefs. "I dated very little because it just didn't feel right," she said.

But the Lord answered her prayer when she met Bob. "He was exactly the one I had been praying for," she continued. "I fell head over heels in love with him. Bob had lost his wife after 39 years of marriage."

If I choose to date again, please do not condemn me for wanting companionship and, yes, love. For wanting someone to sit with me in the evening as we share our day over hot cups of coffee. Someone who likes my broccoli casserole. Someone who can make me laugh again . . . and who will laugh with me. Someone to hold me and reassure me that we are going to make it.

"...if two lie down together, they will keep warm. But how can one keep warm alone?"
Ecclesiastes 4:11 (NIV)

++++++++++++++++++++

Meet Numbness, my best friend.

The "firsts" that strike again and again in the widowhood club are extremely difficult. But, as hard as it may be for you to understand, "seconds" can be even tougher to face. Please lift me up for strength and courage to face these steps as I move through my months and perhaps years as a widow.

Entrance into the widowhood club was immediately marked by an instant world of heart wrenching "firsts" for Kay: first Christmas, first birthday, first anniversary, first meal, first winter, first time changing a tire…so many firsts without her husband.

But a strange phenomenon occurred: the second year without him was harder than the first. How was that possible? The answer was simple in its complexity. The first year of loss was thankfully covered with a blanket of numbness, indeed, a gift of protection from the Lord. Those raw wounds from her husband's death were bandaged in order to allow her to begin to heal. To try to grasp the full impact of what had occurred caused a tremendous emotional pain.

The numbing sensation became a welcome guest because it allowed her to focus on the immediate responsibilities that she faced: children wanting to be fed, bills demanding to be paid, laundry needing to be washed.

But as the second year began, the numbness quietly slipped away and was replaced with the reality of membership in the club: her husband was really gone and he was not coming back.

So if my first year of membership has seemed to the onlooker to have passed without incident, remember that I am entering a second year without numbness as my constant companion. Please lift me up as I choose strength and courage to take its place.

> "I can do everything through Him
> who gives me strength."
> Philippians 4:13 (NIV)

++++++++++++++++++++++

Sleep, where are you?

Kay found that she had many nights after her husband passed away when she lay wide awake and absolutely could not sleep. On her mind was everything she had done that day plus what she had on her list for the next.

She longed for her husband to be beside her, holding her as he reassured her that everything would be okay. "A lot of nights, no matter what I did, I could not sleep, so I would get down on my knees and cry out to the Lord to help me and He did. I would crawl back in bed and be able to sleep."

If you are unsure what to do for someone who has lost her husband, consider lifting her up every single day that she will have a restful, peaceful sleep through the night. Pray that each worry and fear will be replaced by the sweet sleep that only Jesus can give His children.

> "When you lie down, you will not be afraid;
> When you lie down, your sleep will be sweet."
> Proverbs 3:24 (NIV)

+++++++++++++++++++++

Kay's journey continues . . .

In the summer of 2004, twelve years after becoming a widow, Kay was blessed with meeting a wonderful, polite, fun loving gentleman named Bob. One year later, they were married in an intimate ceremony at Garden of Dreams in Missouri.

"We have given each other strength and companionship and, yes, love," Kay smiles. "Finding Bob after so many years alone was answered prayer."

Together they have weathered many storms: surgeries, cancer treatments, more surgeries and the loss of family and friends. "It has been so comforting to have each other in those hard times."

But they have also shared several praises: the birth of a granddaughter, a blessed marriage of 12 years, traveling and sightseeing together.

"We thank God," Kay shares, "for allowing us to find each other and to share the rest of our lives together. We are blessed."

> "The Lord gives strength to his people;
> the Lord blessed his people with peace."
> Psalm 29:11 (NIV)

++++++++++++++++++++++

Holding on . . .

If you are a widow, can you identify with Kay and the thoughts she has shared? Journal your feelings, thoughts and encouraging Scriptures here.

_____
_____
_____
_____
_____
_____
_____
_____
_____
_____
_____
_____
_____

By her side...

If you are a friend to a widow, can you identify with the help that Kay has shared? Journal your feelings, thoughts and encouraging Scriptures here.

_____

_____

_____

_____

_____

_____

_____

_____

_____

_____

Chapter Six

Linda's journey begins . . .

Psalm 23:1, 3, 4 "The Lord is my shepherd, I shall not want…he restores my soul…Even though I walk through the valley of the shadow of death, I will fear no evil, for you are with me;…" (NIV)

The decision of the jury.

Cancer. Few words can strike more fear into the heart of a human being than that one. Perhaps because one day it is silent and the next, screaming at the top of its lungs. But there it is, in black and white. Tests don't lie. They do not have Linda's name on them, but that of her husband of 48 years. The evidence is presented. And the jury is out only a short time before the verdict is read: "Death," it says. No reduced sentence, no extended time to appeal. It is final. And Linda becomes yet another unwilling member in the club.

"You came near when I called you,
and you said, "Do not fear."
Lamentations 3:57 (NIV)
++++++++++++++++++++++

There's nothing easy here.

The hardest part of being a widow is…being a widow. There is no easy part. "I am not lonely…I am empty," says Linda. "There are so many times when I feel like "what's the use?"

In Linda's kitchen are large pots and pans. She no longer cooks for two. Should she get rid of them? "My loaf of bread and carton of milk spoil. Only one uses them now instead of two. I go to the grocery store and find few food items for one. So I buy more bread and milk and bring them home…so they will spoil."

I am surviving membership in this club I did not choose to join because I am dwelling in the tent of my God.

> "For in the day of trouble he will keep me safe in
> his dwelling; he will hide me in the
> shelter of his tabernacle and set
> me high upon a rock."
> Psalm 27: 5 (NIV)

++++++++++++++++++++

Share it, please!

Please share your memories of my husband with me. I may cry but there is healing in knowing that you, too, remember him and that he lives on in your heart as well as mine.

Linda's husband was an accomplished carpenter and loved making pieces of furniture for people. She says that friends would see her and comment on a shelf or cabinet that her husband had made them and what good work he did.

Still others talked fondly of the hard worker that he was and how he could always be found mowing a lawn or helping someone out without asking for anything in return.

Feel free to share your special memories with me. By saying his name out loud, you are helping to keep his memory alive for his children and grandchildren…and for me.

"I thank my God every time
I remember you."
Philippians 1:3 (NIV)

++++++++++++++++++++

I need a break from the club.

Remember that when you tell me "We will get together soon," I know the chances are slim to none that you will call. So surprise me! You feel badly for me. I see it in your eyes as you hug me during the visitation and at the funeral.

You want more than anything, at that moment, for me to feel better. So you are quick to offer up a glimmer of hope that some sense of normalcy will again be present in my life. "We will get together soon," you whisper. You are being kind and compassionate and you fully intend to do just that. But days roll into weeks into months. And still no contact.

There is a paved road that many travel down. Good intentions are at every crossroad, on every sign. Arriving at the destination is easy. Simply say you will do something and then do not do it. Plan to do it…mean to do it…think about doing it, but do not follow through.

Take a deep breath and call me. Allow ME to buy the cup of coffee. I need to talk. And you need to carry out your good intention.

> "Do not take advantage of a widow or an orphan.
> If you do and they cry out to me, I will
> certainly hear their cry."
> Exodus 22:22-23 (NIV)

++++++++++++++++++++

Don't minimize my membership.

Whether or not you approve of how I am coping with my loss is irrelevant to me. But please do not trivialize my grief. Telling me that "Nobody ever died from grieving" implies that what I am going through is short-lived and therefore unimportant.

Seeing someone grieving tends to make others uncomfortable. And something else occurs: the realization that, sooner or later, we will all meet this same foe…this death.

Someday you will be faced with the same decisions that I am facing: when and how to grieve. This grieving process, for me, may continue for weeks, months or even years.

The separation from my husband is temporary – of that I am sure. But understand that I may grieve until I see him again…on the other side.

"Where, O death, is your victory?
Where, O death, is your sting?"
I Corinthians 15:55 (NIV)

++++++++++++++++++++++

Making every moment count . . .

After the funeral of her husband, Linda found time to reflect over her life. "I was married 48 years," she said. "and I've spent the best years of my life working. How I wish I had spent more time with my husband!"

That is often a natural reaction when losing a loved one - even if the husband and wife have shared a considerable amount of time together in their marriage.

We are not promised one second more," Linda reflects. "Yes, we have careers and daily things we need to do. But we need to make sure we prioritize our time so that we can enjoy and love those who are most dear to us."

> "Why, you do not even know what will happen tomorrow. What is your life? You are a mist that appears for a little while and then vanishes."
> James 4:14 (NIV)

++++++++++++++++++++++

I hate the word "widow". . .

The dictionary definition of "widow" is a woman who has lost her spouse and has not remarried. But it also says that "widow" is the last word of a paragraph falling at the top of a page and considered undesirable. In a way, both definitions describe me.

I have lost my husband, yes. But I also feel, at times, that I have become undesirable to those around me just by the term "widow" itself. Friends who are still couples no longer call as they once did. Even some I have known from church.

Perhaps it is because they are uncertain as to how to treat me and do not want to cause further pain or heartache since they are still couples and not singles. Couples go bowling together. Tennis takes two partners. Even checkers requires more than one to play.

Oh, how I understand that! But please hear my heart: it appears, when you do not call and ask me to go with you as we all once did, that I was accepted as part of a couple but not as a single – a widow.

Please call. I will still hate being single and I certainly will not begin to like the term "widow," but I will love that you want to include me again.

"Religion that God our Father accepts as pure and faultless is this: to look after orphans and widows in their distress and to keep oneself from being polluted by the world."
James 1:27 (NIV)

++++++++++++++++++++

Linda's journey continues...

"Twelve years have passed since my husband Charles went to heaven. I miss him almost as much as I did at the time of his passing," Linda shares.

After her husband's death, Linda worked ten more years before retiring. "Working at my job every day kept me very busy," she said "and so the daytime hours did not seem so empty." But there was no longer her best friend to share the day with when she returned home each evening.

And she quickly realized that chores that were once handled by two became the responsibility of one, which made it difficult to keep up. "There were times when I could not help but ask myself since he's not here, what does it matter?"

Linda is thankful that she is able to pay bills, buy groceries, keep up with tax information and drive herself to appointments. She understands that often widows are not able to do many of those things without assistance from friends or family.

"When people ask me how I am and how I am getting along, I answer "I'm fine." And really I am. But there will always be a part of me missing Charles. I encourage all widows to press on! Life goes on and we must, too."

"I press on toward the goal to win the prize for
which God has called me heavenward
in Christ Jesus."
Philippians 3:14 (NIV)
++++++++++++++++++++

Holding on . . .

If you are a widow, can you identify with Linda and the thoughts she has shared? Journal your feelings, thoughts and encouraging Scriptures here.

_____

_____

_____

_____

_____

_____

_____

_____

_____

_____

By her side...

If you are a friend to a widow, can you identify with the help that Linda has shared? Journal your feelings, thoughts and encouraging Scriptures here.

_____
_____
_____
_____
_____
_____
_____
_____
_____
_____
_____
_____
_____

Chapter Seven

Jo's journey begins . . .

Psalm 46:1-2 "God is our refuge and strength, an ever-present help in trouble. Therefore we will not fear, though the earth give way and the mountains fall into the heart of the sea." (NIV)

When the dream is a nightmare.

Jo was thrown into the widow club when she was almost 27 years old and the mother of two little girls. "You need to get to the hospital right away, Jo!" she was told. "An accident, a car accident. It's not good." There she sat in the hospital room with her husband as he took his last breath and she took her first . . . as a widow. Her mind kept repeating, over and over "This is a dream. It's not really happening." But her eyes were telling her something entirely different. In an instant, her life as she had known it for the last three years was changed forever.

"Peace I leave with you; my peace I give you.
I do not give to you as the world gives. Do not let
your hearts be troubled and do not be afraid."
John 14:27 (NIV)
++++++++++++++++++++++

It's how I cope in the club.

Before Jo and her husband married, they "dated" during the two years he was gone in the service. After he died at the end of October, she fell back into the "he is just away" thinking for a while in an attempt to ease the heartache.

That did not last long, because his friends from the service sent Christmas cards and she had to write again and again about the accident and her husband's death. But it did numb the pain of his loss for a little while.

Please let us cope with this intense sadness in the way we see fit. We are not in denial as to what has occurred with our loss. It will simply allow us to gather strength for the days and months ahead of dealing with the reality of life without our husbands.

> "He gives strength to the weary and increases
> the power of the weak."
> Isaiah 40:29 (NIV)

++++++++++++++++++++

Step out and do something.

Jo says that friends immediately came to her aid after her husband passed away. They had lived in the country on a farm and she knew that she needed to have a farm sale but had no idea where to begin.

"Neighbors in our community were amazing," she says. Some friends were auctioneers who took care of the sale. Others helped her move out of her home in the country and into town. Her sister-in-law watched her daughters so she could go to work. Nothing was asked of Jo in return. People simply saw the need and met the challenge.

The old cliché "If you need anything, just give me a call" might make you feel as if you have helped me, but what if I don't have a phone?

When we see someone hurting, many of us feel the need to "make things better" for that person. That's the easy part. The tough part comes when we make the decision to step out of our perfect, orderly, "normal" world and actually DO something for someone no longer in that organized state. Please put your thoughts into actions.

> "I needed clothes and
> you clothed me, I was sick
> and you looked after me…"
> Matthew 25:36 (NIV)

++++++++++++++++++++

We are in this together.

Realize that I am not the only one hurting in this loss. Consider my husband's parents, siblings, and friends as well as my children and me. We have all sustained battle wounds.

It was extremely hard to see the emotional pain that her in-laws were suffering, Jo said. Well-meaning people tended to focus on the immediate person who had suffered the loss: the wife.

They would go to a sister or brother or parent and ask "How is "she" doing?" without stopping to realize that they are asking that question of someone who is NOT doing any better than "she" is.

A father, a brother, a son, an uncle has died…not just a husband. The loss may not seem as important to you, but it is just as painful to them. Their hopes and dreams for the future with this beloved man have also disappeared with his death.

> "Come to me, all you who
> are weary and burdened, and I
> will give you rest."
> Matthew 11:28 (NIV)

+++++++++++++++++++++++

Is this the new normal?

Jo states that the hardest part of being a widow for her was that her little girls did not have a father. He was gone. He would never see them grow up, graduate, get married. No more playing with his children and then, someday, his grandchildren and great grandchildren.

Her evenings that had previously consisted of her family laughing and loving together now became a time that she spent rocking her daughters and reading to them. And thanking the Lord that her husband lived on in each of their lives.

Allow me to grieve for that which was to be and will never be. For the future that one minute stretched before me with joy and hope and in an instant disappeared forever.

Know that the laughter will come again. Smiles will return one day to our faces. But there is no timetable or schedule that mandates when that must occur.

Watch for it! We may both be surprised.

> "Rejoice with those who rejoice;
> mourn with those who mourn."
> Romans 12:15 (NIV)

++++++++++++++++++++++

I don't need another reason to cry.

Going back to work helped Jo to focus on those people who came to her for help and not on her situation at home. Or at least she thought that was the case. One woman in particular became angry at Jo when she did not help her as quickly and exactly as she wanted.

With a proud toss of her head she informed Jo that she knew why she was a widow: because she was so wicked. Jo drove home and cried. Tears for herself, her small children and her situation. But also, tears for a woman who had intentionally inflicted a wound on her slowly healing heart.

"Sticks and stones may break my bones but words can never harm me" may be a childish chant but please remember that what you say to me in my loss makes a big difference. My heart is already torn in two. I do not need more pain.

> "Reckless words pierce like a sword, but the tongue of the wise brings healing."
> Proverbs 12:18 (NIV)

++++++++++++++++++++

To go or not to go.

If I choose to go to the cemetery often, it's normal. If I choose to go to the cemetery seldom, it's normal. If I choose not to go at all, I am normal.

Jo did not routinely go to the cemetery after her husband died. "I believe that the person is always a part of your life and for me, there was no reason to keep returning to the cemetery," she said.

It may be hard for some to go there and it may be equally hard not to go. If you happen to see any of us sitting beside the gravesite and talking about everything going on in our lives, please do not speculate whether or not we are losing our minds.

We are not. If you notice that we have chosen not to go regularly to the cemetery, again, no speculation is warranted as to our sanity. In either instance, we have chosen the way that brings a sense of comfort, peace and healing for each of us.

> "He is not here; he has risen,
> just as he said."
> Matthew 28:6 (NIV)

++++++++++++++++++++

Jo's journey continues . . .

Looking back over her life, Jo says that God has always been holding her family in the palm of His hand. "There are two sayings – "this too shall pass" and "by the grace of God" – and they are true but we have the responsibility of praying that His will be done and abiding in His decision," she says.

Jo eventually remarried and this year will celebrate fifty-five years together. She states "God has been faithful and has continued to watch over and bless our family. My daughters married Christian men and raised Christian children who married believing mates. All twelve great-grandchildren are involved in Christian activities and learning what the Lord wants in their lives."

It is rewarding to watch the great-grandchildren being faithful in their lives and Jo was able to witness that firsthand. "I had tears in my eyes as I saw our seven year old great-grandson, who had a friend being baptized, grab another friend's hand and walk together to the front of the church to support the other boy. My paternal grandfather, a minister, would be proud to know that the tradition of being faithful continues on in the lives of his relatives."

"One generation will commend your works to another; they will tell of your mighty acts."
Psalm 145:4 (NIV)

+++++++++++++++++++++

Holding on . . .

If you are a widow, can you identify with Jo and the thoughts she has shared? Journal your feelings, thoughts and encouraging Scriptures here.

_____
_____
_____
_____
_____
_____
_____
_____
_____
_____
_____
_____

By her side...

If you are a friend to a widow, can you identify with the help that Jo has shared? Journal your feelings, thoughts and encouraging Scriptures here.

_____

_____

_____

_____

_____

_____

_____

_____

_____

_____

_____

Chapter Eight

Debbie's journey begins . . .

Romans 8:38-39 "For I am convinced that neither death nor life, neither angels nor demons, neither the present nor the future, nor any powers, neither height nor depth, nor anything else in all creation, will be able to separate us from the love of God that is in Christ Jesus our Lord." (NIV)

A dream torn apart.

From the minute the tall, confident, smiling young Army specialist walked into her life, Debbie knew he was the one for her. They had grown up hundreds of miles apart yet had so much in common. The plans each had separately for the future were replaced with one plan together as husband and wife in the service in Kenya. How could they have known that Ken's promise to his lovely wife to grow old and wrinkled together would be shattered by a terrorist bomb one August morning in a foreign country. An explosion of broken dreams, broken lives and a shocking loss escorted Debbie unceremoniously into the widowhood club.

"Have mercy on me, O God,
have mercy on me, for in you my soul
takes refuge. I will take refuge in the
shadow of your wings until the
disaster has passed."
Psalm 57:1 (NIV)

++++++++++++++++++++

Where are you God?

There can be nothing worse than knowing your husband has been killed and you cannot do anything to change that. Except. Except having his death occur while in a foreign country and needing to somehow get your child, you and your belongings back home.

"That night was one of horror. The darkness pressed in from all sides. I was alone and afraid like never before in my life" said Debbie. There would be days turning into weeks of packing belongings for the move back to Missouri.

An officer was assigned the duty of escorting Debbie and her daughter from Kenya to the US. She continued "I asked God, where are you?" and He met me right there in that home on Ngong Road and sheltered me from the crushing weight of grief."

No matter where you are, no matter what situation or circumstance, God is there. Just call His name.

> "Where can I go from your Spirit?
> Where can I flee from your presence?
> If I go up to the heavens, you are there;
> If I make my bed in the depths, you are there."
> Psalm 139:7-8 (NIV)

++++++++++++++++++++++

A gift in the sadness.

Debbie and her daughter moved back to Missouri to comfort her husband's precious parents and family. People came with bags of food and armfuls of hugs, wanting so much to console the grieving family.

"We cried. We mourned and we prayed," said Debbie. She was sick with grief – but something else, too.

A week after her arrival in Missouri, Debbie found out that she was expecting a baby in April. Tears of sadness now intermingled with tears of joy.

Even in the lowest points in our lives, when we feel the weight of loss threatening to crush us, God stays close by. Ready to surprise us with a blessing beyond anything we can imagine.

> ". . . to comfort all who mourn, and provide for
> those who grieve . . . to bestow on them a crown
> of beauty instead of ashes, the oil of gladness
> instead of mourning, and a garment of praise
> instead of a spirit of despair. . ."
> Isaiah 61:2-3 (NIV)

++++++++++++++++++++

Is it too soon?

Many times when a spouse dies, there may be a desire to someday marry again. The closeness of that relationship is missed and a hope exists that a new one might be possible.

After Debbie's daughter was born, she and the major who had accompanied her and her son home from Kenya were married.

"He had seen his share of heartache but he could not get over the misery thrust upon such a young family," Debbie said. "But," she added, "there was so much of the grief process yet to be experienced that had to be worked through in the context of a new marriage."

Counselors often advise not to marry too soon after suffering the loss of a spouse and especially one that is both sudden and traumatic. Time is needed to move throughout the stages of grief and the beginning of healing for the mind and heart.

And while marrying soon after the loss of a spouse can certainly and obviously work out, if you find yourself both working through the loss of a spouse and contemplating beginning a new relationship, I suggest you seek the guidance of a counselor and that you take this before the Lord.

"Be completely humble and gentle;
be patient, bearing with one another in love.
Make every effort to keep the unity of the
Spirit through the bond of peace."
Ephesians 4:2-3 (NIV)

++++++++++++++++++++++

You want me to forgive?

To lose a husband because of disease or at an advanced age or because of an accident is one thing. But to lose your husband because of an intentional desire to kill and destroy calls into question whether or not forgiveness is even possible.

"I will always remember how I was sought after and rescued out of the heart of darkness by the God of the entire Universe," Debbie shares. "He is at work even now to set me aside for His purposes . . . to love the way He loves . . . to forgive the way He has forgiven me."

Debbie continues "To the terrorists who shook my world to the foundations: I forgive you. I pray for your souls. May Jesus meet you in your dreams and awaken you to a new life in Him. He died for you to have assurance of salvation. He is as much yours as mine. Come."

It's not easy, forgiving those who chose to kill your husband. And it takes time. But it is possible. For when you forgive them, you are letting go of anger, bitterness and revenge. And you are allowing God to take over in their lives. Debbie has chosen to forgive, just as she was forgiven.

"Be kind and compassionate to one another, forgiving each other, just as in Christ God forgave you."
Ephesians 4:32 (NIV)

++++++++++++++++++++

Who's afraid of the big bad wolf?

Hate is an evil that attacks without warning and can create fear in anyone who dares to get in its path. Debbie had moved back to the states and had remarried after her first husband was killed in a terrorist attack in Kenya.

But hate did not confine itself to that country. Instead it sneaked into the US and precisely into the Pentagon on 9-11-01. The same building that her new husband was assigned to work. "I immediately got on my knees and prayed and asked God for mercy," she said, "and I wondered if there was any place to run to from this horror."

Hours later, tired and blistered from his march across Arlington, her husband was able to call her on a fellow traveler's cell phone to let her know that he was okay. "We shared the news with friends and family, thanking God for His protection," she said.

There may be days when a widow wonders who is next as fear quietly whispers that threat to her heart. Please understand that she has been dealt a blow of significant proportions with her loss and the temptation might be there to pull those she loves close and never let them go. That feeling will pass. Because God is still in control of everything in the universe – including the big bad wolf.

"The Lord is my light and my salvation – whom shall
I fear? The Lord is the stronghold of my
life – of whom shall I be afraid?"
Psalm 27:1 (NIV)

++++++++++++++++++++++

Trusting that the harness is secure.

Just like a roller coaster ride in an amusement park, life can also take unexpected turns. "The ability to survive or even enjoy the ride," Debbie shares, "rests upon whether or not we are securely strapped in."

And what keeps you from falling? What holds you in place through it all? "Jesus is our harness," Debbie states emphatically. "He straps us in."

Please understand that the sensation of falling won't go away. Just the opposite happens. The mind – and heart – are constantly being "tricked" into thinking that down is up and up never happens. But that is where faith in the One who has His arms securely wrapped around you comes in.

His strength will give you a security and peace in knowing that, whether you are up or down or somewhere in between, God will never let go of you, His precious child.

> "Now faith is being sure of
> what we hope for and certain
> of what we do not see."
> Hebrews 11:1 (NIV)

++++++++++++++++++++++

Debbie's journey continues...

"I think I went through a wilderness experience, if that makes sense," Debbie shares. "Remarriage was hard – so hard. There were times when it felt like the Lord was far away and I was in a dry spiritual wasteland."

But she says she was grateful for the many ways God reached out: a Christian radio station filling their home with worship music and ministry; being part of a loving church family; teaching and ministry opportunities at their church.

"I look back in wonder at how the Lord blessed each baby step of obedience," she continues. She is serving in women's ministry leadership at the American Church in Paris, distributing sandwiches to the homeless and sharing what Jesus meant by walking in the light.

Debbie looks at her experience and encourages each of us: "do not lose heart."

"Therefore, since we are surrounded by such a great cloud of witnesses, let us throw off everything that hinders and the sin that so easily entangles, and let us run with perseverance the race marked out for us. Let us fix our eyes on Jesus, the author and perfecter of our faith, who for the joy set before him endured the cross, scorning its shame."
Hebrews 12:1-2 (NIV)

++++++++++++++++++++++

Holding on . . .

If you are a widow, can you identify with Debbie and the thoughts she has shared? Journal your feelings, thoughts and encouraging Scriptures here.

_____
_____
_____
_____
_____
_____
_____
_____
_____
_____
_____
_____

By her side . . .

If you are a friend to a widow, can you identify with the help that Debbie has shared? Journal your feelings, thoughts and encouraging Scriptures here.

_____
_____
_____
_____
_____
_____
_____
_____
_____
_____
_____
_____

Chapter Nine

Saundra's journey begins...

Philippians 4: 6 "Do not be anxious about anything, but in everything, by prayer and petition, with thanksgiving, present your requests to God." (NIV)

Nothing you could do?

Saundra had not even the slightest clue of her imminent initiation into the widowhood club. She and her husband had been married 28 years and he was a sports enthusiast and physically active. They had eaten out with friends one evening and had had a wonderful time of laughter and conversation. Later in the night, she awoke to her husband saying "I am really sick. You need to take me to the hospital," which she did immediately. She found herself sitting, alone, in the hospital waiting area, thinking "The flu? Something he ate? I wonder what is wrong?" and praying with all her might. She had no idea that, a few minutes later, a doctor would come out and say "I'm sorry. It was his heart. There was nothing we could do. He's gone." Her immediate club initiation was followed by "Okay, we need his social security number, insurance papers, those things." She could only stare. "You need what? You just told me my husband has died! MY husband! MY soulmate! MY security! MY life! And you want what?" Thus her journey began into the unchartered territory known as "The Widow."

> "The Lord is close to the brokenhearted
> and saves those who are
> crushed in spirit."
> Psalm 34:18 (NIV)

++++++++++++++++++++

I no longer dance.

There is no question that you still have your dance partner and I do not. Please refrain from telling me as you spin and twirl around the dance floor why you think . . .

"It's better this way."

"I know how you feel."

"At least he didn't suffer."

"Life will go on."

"It will get better with time."

"You'll get married again someday."

"There will be better days ahead."

"You had more years together than most people."

"If you only had MY husband, you wouldn't be so sad."

Perhaps some of those statements are true, perhaps not. Regardless, I only want to know that you are praying for me and I want YOU to know that I will remember to never utter even one of those statements when you lose your dance partner one day.

"But I tell you that men will have to give account
on the day of judgment for every
careless word they have spoken."
Matthew 12:36 (NIV)

++++++++++++++++++++++

Sometimes I need to vent.

"Do not sound the alarm if you walk by my home and hear me yelling my husband's name at the top of my lungs," shares Saundra. "I am not going crazy nor am I hallucinating. I am just venting."

Please allow me to be frustrated that there are some things he could fix and some that I could not…and still can't! The car breaks down. I get it repaired. It breaks down again. It is repaired again…maybe. The zipper is caught halfway up in the back of my dress and I am late. The electricity is off because of the storm and I cannot find the circuit breaker box. Or a candle.

The phone rings for the fourth time and no one is there. The road map makes no sense and I am lost. "Do I mix one part oil with two parts gas or the other way around for my weed eater?" I think to myself. I feel really sick. What if it is serious? Do I go to the doctor? What is that sound? Could someone be in my home?

I am not helpless. I am just struggling as I try to deal with all the things my husband automatically handled. Do not make light of my club membership. After I learn how to take care of these things (and I WILL learn), you may someday need to call on me for help. And I will be ready.

"In my distress I called to the Lord;
I cried to my God for help. From his temple
he heard my voice; my cry came
before him, into his ears."
Psalm 18:6 (NIV)

+++++++++++++++++++++

A time to cry.

While a widow can talk with you about her loss, she may also need to talk with a counselor and certainly with The Counselor as she heals.

Her daughter delivered her first grandchild almost four years to the day after Saundra joined the club. "My husband was gone; my security was gone," she said. "Faith was replaced with fear. Fear that something might be wrong with the baby or my daughter," she continued.

A feeling of panic began to slowly creep through her body until it threatened to suffocate her every waking moment. "Who will be next?" Satan whispered with each passing day.

She decided to go to a Christian counselor. What she learned was that she had been so busy consoling others, taking care of all the necessary paperwork surrounding this loss and continuing to work at her job, that she had neglected one very important thing: she hadn't grieved. She also found that she was afraid. Afraid that if she truly "let herself go" and cried over the loss of her husband, she wouldn't be able to stop crying.

Her wise counselor suggested she set a time to cry. That may sound preplanned or packaged to you. But in Ecclesiastes 3:4, we are told there is "a time to weep and a time to laugh, a time to mourn and a time to dance." She planned a time to weep. And weep she did. Again and again. But with each time came healing and a comfort and peace from our Wonderful Counselor that one day, there would also be a time to laugh.

"Hear my cry, O God, listen to my prayer. From the
ends of the earth I call to you. I call as my
heart grows faint; lead me to the
rock that is higher than I."
Psalm 61:1-2 (NIV)
+++++++++++++++++++++

Together and yet alone.

The membership in the "Widowhood Club" is in the millions. Yet standing shoulder to shoulder, we can feel very alone.

I will continue for a very long time to turn and look for my husband at my side. But I will be alone. Alone in a crowd, alone at home, alone at church, alone when I go out to eat. And even though my head knows I will not see him, my heart will continue to look for him.

I will also continue: to sleep on his side of the bed. To put his cologne on his pillow. To keep some of his clothes in the closet. To feel my heart skip a beat when I see a truck like his. To look up from my paper and expect him to be smiling at me from his.

If I had chosen this…aloneness…then you would not be obligated to feel sympathy for me. But this was not of my doing OR my choice…So continue to pray for me as I struggle through this desolate, lonely place known as "The Widowhood."

"pray continually;"
I Thessalonians 5:17 (NIV)
+++++++++++++++++++++

Please don't forget.

Being driven to the funeral home the day of her husband's service gave Saundra time to reflect on what had happened and what lay ahead. But she found herself staring out the car window. "Look at all these people!" she thought. "They are going about their business as if everything is okay. Do they not know that my world is devastated? Don't they know this is the day of Kenny's funeral?"

Once the initial shock of loss is over, people tend to return to their pre-loss lives. Sympathy cards that arrived by the hundreds are soon replaced by bills and credit card promotions. "How are you doing?" phone calls are replaced with silence.

Your life will go on as usual after my loss. Do not assume that mine will do the same. Because it will not.

Please do not forget us! As Christians we know who holds tomorrow. And, as Paul Harvey says, "… (we) know the rest of the story." We do not mourn as the rest of the world, but we ARE mourning. Just continue, in the weeks and months ahead, to let us know that you care.

> "I tell you the truth, you will weep and
> mourn while the world rejoices.
> You will grieve, but your
> grief will turn to joy."
> John 16:20 (NIV)

++++++++++++++++++++++++

The grass is not invisible.

Saundra was in her yard when a man from church came to see her. As he stood in the 8 inch tall grass, he said "If I can do anything at all, just let me know."

She thought to herself "I need my lawn mowed. You are standing in the middle of a need that I have. If you cannot see it, maybe it's not something you want to do for me."

So she thanked him but said nothing else. And he left thinking that all was well.

Perhaps it's a desire to be independent that prevents us from sharing our needs with you. Perhaps it is pride. Maybe it is simply that we do not want to take you away from your family and their needs.

Whatever the answer, please know that if you will simply open the eyes of your heart, the Lord will make clear to you what needs a widow has and what you can do to help her. He will also encourage you to pause and wait for her answer…and not leave the tall grass unattended.

> "Each of you should look not only to your own interests, but also to the interests of others."
> Philippians 2:4 (NIV)

+++++++++++++++++++++

Saundra's journey continues...

Saundra continued to work outside the home until 2008. Now she keeps busy serving as a volunteer at her local hospital, as prayer chairperson for her church and as treasurer of Lamar Area Christian Ministries. She also belongs to a widows group. They meet every Wednesday to share lunch and encouragement with each other.

Her mother will soon turn 100 years young and Saundra is her driver to the doctor and grocery store. She also likes to visit at least once a month at her daughter's home.

"I have become comfortable with widowhood by God's strength and provision," Saundra shares. "There will always be an empty space in my life where my husband was but when loneliness comes, I get busy with other people and their challenges. God has truly blessed me. My identity is in the Lord, nothing else."

> "I have been crucified with Christ and I no longer live
> but Christ lives in me. The life I live in the body,
> I live by faith in the Son of God, who
> loved me and gave himself for me."
> Galatians 2:20 (NIV)

++++++++++++++++++++

Holding on . . .

If you are a widow, can you identify with Saundra and the thoughts she has shared? Journal your feelings, thoughts and encouraging Scriptures here.

By her side . . .

If you are a friend to a widow, can you identify with the help that Saundra has shared? Journal your feelings, thoughts and encouraging Scriptures here.

_____
_____
_____
_____
_____
_____
_____
_____
_____
_____
_____

Chapter Ten

Jan's journey begins . . .

Psalm 116:15 "Precious in the sight of the Lord is the death of his saints." (NIV)

Two become one.

When Jan and her husband Allen met one July, it was almost instant chemistry, as the saying goes. They knew each other's thoughts and words before they were even spoken and by July of the next year, they were husband and wife. They shared a love of coffee and would spend almost every evening after they were married sitting side by side with cups of the hot liquid, speaking very little, completely satisfied just being together. But those special moments came to an abrupt end when Allen had sudden severe pain and a hospital emergency room visit revealed the unthinkable: cancer. Everywhere. Only five months later, to the day, Jan whispered "I love you" to her best friend as he stepped before the Lord and she stepped into her new role as a widow.

"Record my lament; list my tears
On your scroll – are they not in your record?"

Psalm 56:8 (NIV)

+++++++++++++++++++++

Small things can be big.

Cleaning out a bedroom closet is a small thing – unless you are removing clothes after your husband has passed away. It took Jan two years to finally move her husband's things out of their closet and into their bedroom, where they still remain. A little thing to most but not to Jan. Why is that? Because it represents the finality of a lifetime of love. Those clothes won't be worn again by her husband. "Am I normal to do that?" Jan wonders aloud.

Eating out is a small thing. Unless. Unless that special time of eating out together as a couple has become a single, eating alone. It took almost three years for Jan to go to a restaurant by herself. Jan wonders again if she is normal to have taken so long to do the "small" things.

Please understand that "small" for some can be big for a widow. Do not worry about me if you visit my home and notice that my husband's clothes are still folded in my bedroom. Or if you see me eating out but struggling with every bite.

I AM normal. I am just learning to take steps that may seem simple for you but are difficult for me as I travel on this journey. Some days I may run; other days will be a victory when I merely walk. But big or small, the Lord is with me every single step.

"but those who hope in the Lord will renew their strength.
They will soar on wings like eagles; they will
run and not grow weary, they will
walk and not be faint."
Isaiah 40:31 (NIV)

++++++++++++++++++++

Never abandoned.

Jan and her husband have three beautiful children. They became part of their "forever" family at ages 22 months, 32 months and 6 years old. Since they had been abandoned by their biological parents, Jan feared that as young adults they might once again experience the feeling of abandonment at the loss of their father.

One may believe that losing a parent as an adult is easier than as a child. And that may be true to some extent. But consider the fact that the majority of their lives were spent with the man who taught them how to ride bicycles, took them for airplane rides on his shoulders and listened to every thought and idea that they had. The one dad they knew and loved tremendously. Because he was the father who chose them.

Others surely have similar life stories of adoption and love. Please lift up each child, no matter the age, who is grieving over the loss of a "forever" father.

"I will not leave you as orphans; I will come to you."
John 14:18 (NIV)

++++++++++++++++++++

Missing him and missing me.

The dictionary defines the word "miss" as "to notice or feel the absence of someone or something." That to me is such a dry, unemotional description of my loss.

What do I miss? His laughter that made everyone around him smile; his wisdom and patience as he explained to me how to run the lawnmower for the fourth time; his face as he teased me, hoping for a response; his voice, soft and low.

I miss him beside me at night, snoring and then telling me in the morning that it was me. I miss our hot cups of coffee on the patio each evening. I miss his strong arms wrapped around me, just because. Him. I miss him.

And I miss me. The me who laughed at his jokes and asked his opinion on major decisions that needed to be made. The me who never worried because I knew he had the answers. The me who couldn't wait for him to come home from his job so that I could hug him but who sometimes had to stand in line behind three children as they welcomed their daddy home. Me. I miss me.

Please be lifting me up in prayer through this time of missing. A day will come when I will find myself again. Perhaps it is just around the corner. Someone will recall a joke he had told and I will smile. And laugh. Maybe I will even remember his lesson about the lawnmower. But until then I will continue to miss. Him.

"My soul is weary with sorrow; strengthen me according to your word."
Psalm 119:28 (NIV)
++++++++++++++++++++++

When the unexpected becomes the blessing.

Becoming a grandparent is almost always met with excitement and hugs when the announcement is made. For Jan and her husband, hearing that news from their single daughter was not at all what they expected. But their immediate response was one of love and acceptance. "There is always a plan in everything," they told her. "We know that this baby will be a blessing." And blessing he was!

Because not long after the birth of their grandson, Jan's husband became ill and received his diagnosis of cancer. In those weeks of treatments and hospital visits, there were always the smiles and giggles of his grandson to instantly lift his spirits. With this little one came the joy and excitement of new life and renewed hope in the middle of extreme anxiety with each doctor appointment.

"After my husband passed away and we had the funeral, lives began returning to normal – whatever that is," Jan commented. "I was so thankful that my new normal routine included my precious grandson. I could snuggle with him and tell him about his wonderful grandpa who loved him very much."

Being able to focus on her young grandson and his needs helped Jan to be able to get through many of the days ahead. Unexpected? Yes. But a blessing beyond belief.

"And we know that in all things God works for the good of those who love him, who have been called according to his purpose."
Romans 8:28 (NIV)

++++++++++++++++++++++

The Grand Tour.

"What do you suppose heaven looks like?" Jan asked her husband one evening as they were relaxing in front of the television. "I don't know," he grinned at her, "but I DO know that I want to be sure to take the Grand Tour!" She smiled back. "What a great way to think of heaven," she thought.

Not once did she consider that his statement would be coming true in a very short time. But it did, just a few months later.

As the end of her husband's life drew near, Jan sat beside his hospital bed, gently holding his hand. Exhausted, she carefully laid her head down on the cool sheets surrounding him and closed her eyes. She opened them just a few minutes later to the realization that he was gone.

Jan tenderly leaned over to her husband and whispered "Honey, are you taking that Grand Tour?"

Jesus tells us that He is preparing a mansion for us and when it is completed, He will come to take us to heaven. Christ Himself is meeting us face to face. He wants to personally welcome us to our eternal home with Him!

It seems to me that if Jesus is that involved in preparing my home in heaven and then in meeting me face to face, He surely is the one giving the Grand Tour.

"Do not let your hearts be troubled. Trust in God; trust also in me. In my Father's house are many rooms; if it were not so, I would have told you. I am going there to prepare a place for you."
John 14:1-2 (NIV)

++++++++++++++++++++++

Lean on me.

Jan's husband was a huge part of so many lives. His children consulted him daily for his wisdom and opinions. His grandson couldn't wait to be held high in the air in those big secure hands. His wife believed he might actually walk on water. And his father-in-law?

His father-in-law became a father figure to him since his own father had passed away when he was only 19. They worked together for about 20 years, every day, building houses and working in the fields. They also shared an unspoken mutual respect for each other. A bond between a father and a son.

The summer before her husband became ill, Jan recalls his concern for her dad. "He told me that he was worried about Daddy having to be out in the heat in the summer as they worked in the hayfields together. So he made sure to learn how to do every part of the farming operation so that he could do it by himself the next year. We never even thought about this being his last summer with us."

You have seen our faces. You know how much we all depended on this larger-than-life man that we loved so deeply. So you must know that there are many days that we feel lost as to what to do next.

We know that the Lord is with us every day but we also need you as friends and extended family to come around us and be willing to be a part of our lives in the same way that our loved one did.

As we lean on the Lord for strength, can we also lean on you for help?

"So do not fear, for I am with you; do not be
dismayed, for I am your God. I will strengthen you
and help you; I will uphold you with
my righteous right hand."
Isaiah 41:10 (NIV)

++++++++++++++++++++++

Jan's journey continues . . .

"It has been seven years since I lost my 'rock,' my husband," Jan shares. "My children and I have good days mixed in with the not so good. But I am blessed with four grandchildren now and they keep me busy every single day."

Jan prays each night, asking the Lord to give her strength for the next day. "It isn't easy. You are half of a whole. You can put on a face for the world, but when it is just you and God, you don't have to put that face on. He knows how you feel and what you are going through."

Jan says that she would never make it through a single day without God beside her, giving her strength and courage and reminding her that she am not alone.

"Let the morning bring me word of your unfailing love,
for I have put my trust in you. Show me
the way I should go, for to you
I lift up my soul."
Psalm 143:8 (NIV)

++++++++++++++++++++

Holding on . . .

If you are a widow, can you identify with Jan and the thoughts she has shared? Journal your feelings, thoughts and encouraging Scriptures here.

_____
_____
_____
_____
_____
_____
_____
_____
_____
_____

By her side . . .

If you are a friend to a widow, can you identify with the help that Jan has shared? Journal your feelings, thoughts and encouraging Scriptures here.

_____
_____
_____
_____
_____
_____
_____
_____
_____
_____
_____
_____
_____

Conclusion

So there you have it: ten women in a club of millions. Ten women who know what it is like to be thrown in the pit of widowhood and what it is like to survive as they climb out of that pit. The lessons to be learned from each chapter in this book are as varied and unique as the women who present them, yet the similarities remain: all ten women are grieving, all are normal in how they face their loss, and all are holding onto the One who will never let go of them.

Whether a woman has been suddenly thrown into the club or has experienced a gradual descent into its membership, the moment of initiation can cause an overwhelming loss of security and saneness because her world has been shaken to its very depths.

Everything that she has known up to that moment as safe is rocked with the force of an earthquake and she cannot stand against the quake or the aftershocks. The one who protected her and gave her the self-confidence to do anything, the one who was her defense from the world, the one who would have scooped her up and taken her to the place where the quake could not reach…that one – her husband - is gone.

And where was our Father when these ladies were being thrown into the pit of the widow club? Where was He when they were crying out for rescue from this membership? He was crying with them. He was holding out His arms to them. He was whispering their names. He was reassuring them "Never will I leave you; never will I forsake you." Hebrews 13:5 (NIV) And He was quietly reminding them that He DOES have a plan in all the heartache and that He is STILL in control.

We may not like life as a widow right now. But therein lays the key: we don't HAVE to like it. What we need to do...what we MUST do...is trust the One who made us. Trust the One who died for us. Trust the One who whispers OUR names in the middle of this horrible storm that batters us around and threatens to leave our hearts bruised and bleeding. And we need to praise Him - for His love, for His mercy, and for His peace in the middle of this trial.

Where is God when your storm hits? When the winds knock you to your knees and the suffocating force of the situation threatens to drown you in the pit of widowhood? He is there...in the middle of the storm...by your side. He is the Voice that whispers "Hold onto me! We will get through this!" He is the Thunder that shouts "Give me your hand and I will PULL you through!" He is the Father who weeps as you weep, who holds you in His arms. He is the One who wipes the tears from your eyes and repeats, over and over, "I have a plan. Trust me with everything you have and I will give you everything you need." And how could He possibly know how we feel? Because He has been there. Because He watched His Son take His last breath, watched His eyes close in death. Because just as He raised His son Jesus from the grave, He will do no less for His children.

We encourage all of you to stand firm and hold tight to our Father! The grieving may continue for months or years but the words of our Father will continue for eternity. Do you feel like your strength is almost gone? Psalm 73:23-24 (NIV) says "Yet I am always with you; you hold me by my right hand. You guide me with your counsel…" Are there moments when it seems that no one wants to listen to your sadness? Psalm 62:8 (NIV): "Trust in him at all times, O people; pour out your hearts to him, for God is our refuge."

Do you need a place to hide when the pain of your loss threatens to overwhelm you? Consider Psalm 91:1-2 (NIV): "He who dwells in the shelter of the Most High will rest in the shadow of the Almighty. I will say of the Lord, "He is my refuge and my fortress, my God, in whom I trust." Does it seem like no one hears your cry for help? Read Psalm 40: 1-2 (NIV): "I waited patiently for the Lord; he turned to me and heard my cry. He lifted me out of the slimy pit, out of the mud and mire; he set my feet on a rock and gave me a firm place to stand."

We are survivors in a club not of our choosing. It is our prayer that those of you who have joined the ranks of widowhood or who will someday become members as we are will never lose sight of the One who will guide you through. May you find comfort and compassion in His words of encouragement and love as you travel this path as a member of "The Widowhood Club."

"But those who hope in the Lord will renew their strength.
They will soar on wings like eagles; they will run and not grow
weary,
they will walk and not be faint."
Isaiah 40:31 (NIV)

Scripture References

1. Exodus 22:22-23 (NIV)
2. Deuteronomy 31:8 (NIV)
3. Joshua 1:9 (NIV)
4. I Samuel 16:7 (NIV)
5. Psalm 18:2 (NIV)
6. Psalm 18:6 (NIV)
7. Psalm 18:28 (NIV)
8. Psalm 23:1, 3, 4 (NIV)
9. Psalm 27:1 (NIV)
10. Psalm 27:5 (NIV)
11. Psalm 29:11 (NIV)
12. Psalm 30:5b (NIV)
13. Psalm 34:18 (NIV)
14. Psalm 46:1-2 (NIV)
15. Psalm 56:8 (NIV)
16. Psalm 57:1 (NIV)
17. Psalm 61:1-2 (NIV)
18. Psalm 68:5 (NIV)
19. Psalm 73:26 (NIV)
20. Psalm 86:6 (NIV)
21. Psalm 91:1 (NIV)
22. Psalm 91:4 (NIV)
23. Psalm 116:15 (NIV)
24. Psalm 119:28 (NIV)
25. Psalm 139:7-8 (NIV)
26. Psalm 139:23 (NIV)
27. Psalm 143:8 (NIV)
28. Psalm 145:4 (NIV)
29. Psalm 147:3 (NIV)
30. Proverbs 3:5-6 (NIV)
31. Proverbs 3:24 (NIV)
32. Proverbs 12:18 (NIV)
33. Proverbs 14:13 (NIV)
34. Proverbs 15:30 (NIV)
35. Proverbs 18:10 (NIV)
36. Proverbs 18:24 (NIV)

37. Proverbs 21:13 (NIV)
38. Proverbs 31:25 (NIV)
39. Ecclesiastes 4:9-10 (NIV)
40. Ecclesiastes 4:11 (NIV)
41. Ecclesiastes 5:2 (NIV)
42. Song of Solomon 2:8-17 (NIV)
43. Isaiah 40:29 (NIV)
44. Isaiah 40:31 (NIV)
45. Isaiah 41:10 (NIV)
46. Isaiah 41:13 (NIV)
47. Isaiah 61:1 (NIV)
48. Isaiah 61:2-3 (NIV)
49. Jeremiah 29:11 (NIV)
50. Lamentations 3:57 (NIV)
51. Matthew 5:4 (NIV)
52. Matthew 7:7 (NIV)
53. Matthew 8:26 (NIV)
54. Matthew 11:28 (NIV)
55. Matthew 12:36 (NIV)
56. Matthew 25:36 (NIV)
57. Matthew 28:6 (NIV)
58. John 4:13, 14a (NIV)
59. John 6:68 (NIV)
60. John 14:1-2 (NIV)
61. John 14:18 (NIV)
62. John 14:27 (NIV)
63. John 16:20 (NIV)
64. Romans 8:28 (NIV)
65. Romans 8:38-39 (NIV)
66. Romans 9:2 (NIV)
67. Romans 12:15 (NIV)
68. I Corinthians 1:20 (NIV)
69. I Corinthians 15:51-52 (NIV)
70. I Corinthians 15:55 (NIV)
71. II Corinthians 1:4 (NIV)
72. Galatians 2:20 (NIV)
73. Ephesians 1:16 (NIV)
74. Ephesians 4:2-3 (NIV)
75. Ephesians 4:32 (NIV)

76. Philippians 1:3 (NIV)
77. Philippians 1:6 (NIV)
78. Philippians 2:4 (NIV)
79. Philippians 3:14 (NIV)
80. Philippians 4:6 (NIV)
81. Philippians 4:13 (NIV)
82. Colossians 3:12 (NIV)
83. I Thessalonians 5:17 (NIV)
84. I Timothy 5:4 (NIV)
85. Hebrews 4:16 (NIV)
86. Hebrews 11:1 (NIV)
87. Hebrews 12:1-2 (NIV)
88. James 1:27 (NIV)
89. James 4:14 (NIV)
90. Revelation 21:4 (NIV)

www.ingramcontent.com/pod-product-compliance
Lightning Source LLC
LaVergne TN
LVHW051522070426
835507LV00023B/3254